PONDEROSA Country

a scenic and
historic guide to
Reno and vicinity

by Stanley W. Paher

Nevada Publications
Box 15444
Las Vegas, Nevada

Cover Photos

High in the Sierra Nevada and reposed in a framework of immense fir and Western yellow pine, Lake Tahoe and Emerald Bay are captured in the splendid cover photograph by renowned photographer David Muench. The back cover painting showing the magnificent gothic wood-frame house of Theodore Winters was drawn by well known Reno artist Lyle V. Ball.

Printed in the United States of America

Soft cover edition $1.95. Hard cover edition $4.95.

Library of Congress Card Number 72-87135

Nevada Publications
Box 15444
Las Vegas, Nevada 89114

Table of Contents

Acknowledgments

A special thanks goes to Gabriel Vogliotti, who provided substantive editorial assistance with both the text and the picture captions. On numerous occasions Florence Lee Cahlan gave general assistance to the preparation of this book.

Interviews with Silas E. Ross and Amy Gulling brought many interesting and useful facts to light. Technical assistance of various kinds also came from K. C. Den Dooven, Roy Purcell, Cliff Nakatani, and John F. Cahlan.

Dr. James R. Herz, an untiring collector of Nevada memorabilia, generously loaned many rare photographs to this project. Pamela Crowell's help with pictures at the Nevada State Museum is worthy of special mention, as is Robert D. Armstrong's at the University of Nevada at Reno.

Other photo credits are as follows: (An "a" denotes a picture on the top of a page; "b" and "c" are those in descending order. Numerals in parenthesis designate the quantity of pictures on the page.)

Chester Barton, 9b, 11, 12b and c. Norman Biltz, 38. Mrs. Jack Burns, 12a, 13a and c. Willie Capucci, 43(2), 44(2), 47(2). Pete Gavazzi, 35a. Amy Gulling, 30a, 35b. Dr. James Herz, 40(2), 41(3), 46(2). Library of Congress, 20(3), 21(3), 24a. Thomas W. Miller, 36a. Frank Mitrani photo, 22, 23(2). David Muench photo, 15, cover. Myrtle T. Myles, 36b. Nevada State Historical Society, 10b, 45b. Nevada State Museum, 9, 10a, 16, 17(2), 25b, inside front cover. Mrs. R. R. Purdy, 27a, 37. Reno Chamber of Commerce, 33b, 48, inside back cover. University of Nevada, Reno, Special Collections Department, 31b, 34a. United States Geological Survey, 6. John Zalac, 18, 42(2).

ALSO BY STANLEY W. PAHER

Nevada Ghost Towns & Mining Camps

Northwestern Arizona Ghost Towns

Las Vegas, As it began, as it grew

Death Valley Teamsters

Death Valley Ghost Towns

Introduction

Within an hour or two of Reno are many scenic byways and colorful spots with unexplored charm.

Many visitors to "The Biggest Little City" arrive and depart without straying from the downtown area. True, the glittering "Casino Row" has great attraction—but there are amazingly attractive points in the immediate area, too.

Stanley Paher, one of the most knowledgable of Nevada writers, has put together an interesting handbook as a guide to this area. He organizes a series of four tours—one for every direction of the compass—in which you are guided to several dozen worthwhile places to visit. More than five dozen photographic illustrations culled from many collections help explain the historic and scenic significance of these sites.

The last third of the book is a pictorial history of Reno itself. The City typifies the spirit of lusty Nevada. Born on May 9, 1868, as the first fruit of the Central Pacific Railroad's eastward march, Reno immediately became a frontier boom town. It thrived on the immense amount of freighting activity from its railroad depot to nearby points, especially the mining camp of Virginia City. In the current century, Reno gained new fame through divorces, legal gambling and now as a recreation capital.

Stanley Paher is best known for his big Western classic, *Nevada Ghost Towns & Mining Camps*, which was published in 1970. It was given the coveted Award of Merit by the American Association of State & Local History.

For the last several years, since his student days at University of Nevada, Reno, Stanley Paher has been collecting data about Reno, interviewing old-timers, and borrowing pictorial evidence of Reno's varied history. I'm sure he has a detailed history of Reno as an ultimate objective. Perhaps it will match his successful *Las Vegas, As It Began, As It Grew*, released in late 1971. With this goal in mind, Paher is increasing his efforts to correspond with individuals possessing old diaries, letters, and especially old photos that depict Reno life as it was 30, 60 and even 90 years ago. So dig in that attic trunk or bureau drawer and see what you have.

October 1972
Nevada State Journal   Ty Cobb

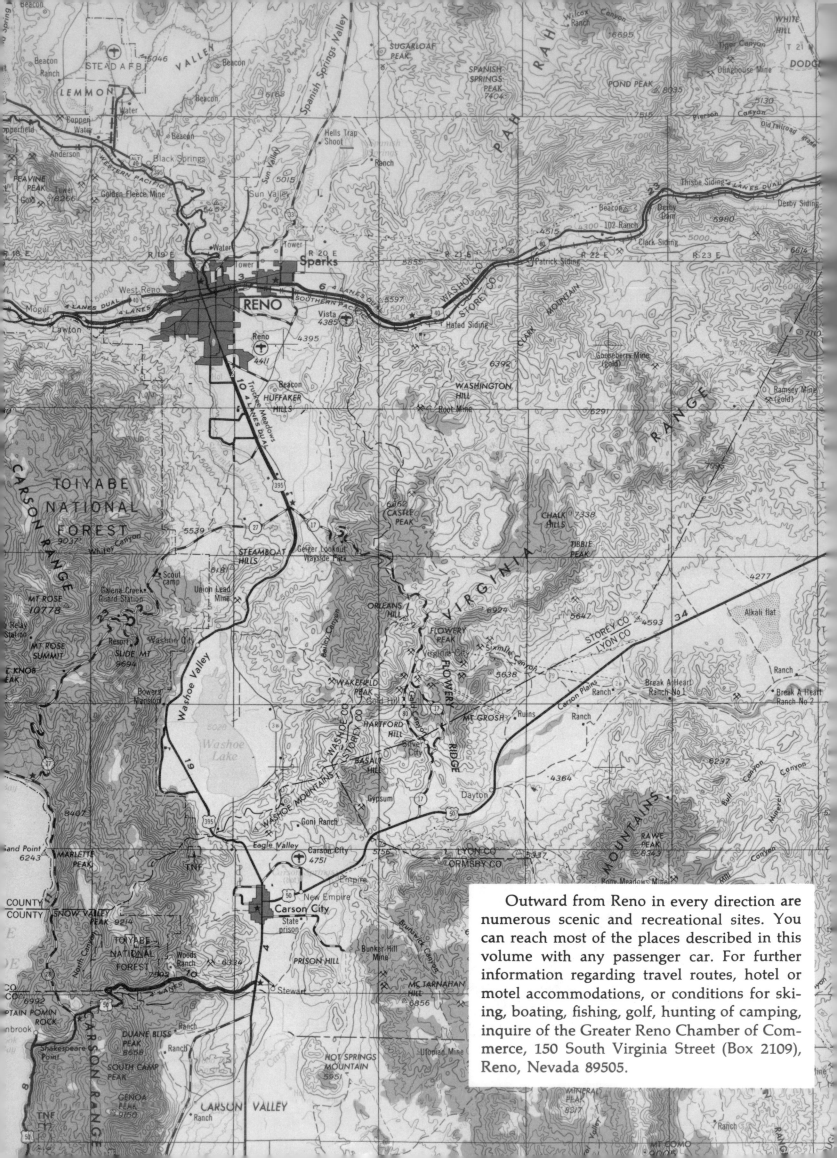

Outward from Reno in every direction are numerous scenic and recreational sites. You can reach most of the places described in this volume with any passenger car. For further information regarding travel routes, hotel or motel accommodations, or conditions for skiing, boating, fishing, golf, hunting of camping, inquire of the Greater Reno Chamber of Commerce, 150 South Virginia Street (Box 2109), Reno, Nevada 89505.

Bonanza Tour: South of Reno

Scenic spots are at almost every turn of the 29 miles of US 395 from Reno to Carson City. Small ranches are at the southern outskirts of Reno as soon as you leave the business district. In this area, the rolling foothills of the Sierra Nevada slope down to meet the south end of the Truckee Meadows. Early settlements made before 1860 were at such places as Junction House, three miles south of downtown Reno, as at Huffaker's Station, two miles farther on. The site of Junction House has a historical marker, while a stone building, once used as a store, remains at Huffaker's. Both are among the oldest settlements in Nevada.

There is an important junction 9-½ miles south of downtown Reno. To the right, State Route 27 starts a gentle climb westward to the Slide Mountain ski resorts and to the enormous Lake Tahoe complex. To the left, State Route 17 to Virginia City ascends eastward where it disappears into a high mountain range. That road's many bends give some of the more spectacular views of the West (see page 18).

From 11 to 12 miles south of Reno (on US 395) are the well-known Steamboat Springs, which are fissures and crevices in rock that give off dense clouds of steam. Fissures occur on both sides of the road for nearly a mile. California-bound emigrants camped at the springs as early as 1849. The first permanent settler came about 1860 and ever since then some sort of resort use has been made of the unusual hot water.

US 395 next goes through the fertile pleasant valley, which was settled by Mormon farmers around 1855, and then tops a low summit to enter Washoe Valley. Two lakes, Little Washoe and Washoe, appear on the left, and 16 miles south of Reno is the ghost town of Washoe City.

In the 1860's Washoe City was an important lumbering and silver milling town which thrived because of early mining activity at Virginia City. It was the first seat of Washoe County before Reno won the distinction in 1871. In the mid-1860's several thousand people lived in the valley. Washoe City's saloons saw many fights and shootings involving the local woodcutters and bullwhackers and Virginia City's miners and teamsters. The last commercial remnant, a solitary stone building, is on the east side of US 395, while on the west side a little farther south is a well preserved cemetery.

After this point, US 395 soon becomes a freeway. The older parallel route is still used and leads to historic points. In a private field about a quarter mile west of the highway and 20 miles south of Reno are the fallen walls of the huge Ophir silver mill. Slightly west is the site of Ophir City, now partially obliterated by freeway construction. In the 1860's that village had a post office, stores, lawyers' offices, saloons, and immense wagon yards.

Another mile or so, 21 miles from Reno and beyond two sweeping turns of the highway, is the Bowers Mansion, still partially hidden by tall Lombardy poplars. It was built in the 1860's by the Comstock millionaire, Sandy Bowers, for his wife, the former Eilley Orrum. The square two-story sandstone building and surrounding grounds are now operated by Washoe County as a public park and museum. There is a small admission fee to enter the building.

After leaving Washoe Valley, US 395 crosses a low pass called Lakeview Summit, named because of the view of Washoe Lake, not Tahoe. Eagle Valley and Carson City come into view as you descend from Lakeview Summit. Visible on the hillside to the west is the abandoned grade of the famed Virginia & Truckee Railroad, which once operated from Reno to Carson City and up the steep grade to Virginia City.

As a symbol of millionaire status, Sandy and Eilley Bowers in 1864 built this 16-room mansion with a pale and symmetrical facade. Note the flags draped on the building and the coach. The occasion is said to be the Bowers' departure over the Sierra to meet Queen Victoria in San Francisco.

Carson City

The settlement of Nevada's capital city dates back to November 1851 when a band of tired California gold seekers saw the lush Eagle Valley and stayed to start a trading post and a ranch. By September 1858 a group headed by Abraham Curry laid out a townsite; it provided for wide streets and a four-square-block plaza for town meetings and auctions. The town founders offered free lots to anyone who would build on them.

When the Territory of Nevada was created in 1861, its legislators chose Carson City as the capital. It retained the distinction when Nevada became a state three years later. During that decade the legislators met in various places, including Curry's Warm Springs Hotel at the present site of the state penitentiary, two miles east of town. In one session they chose the plaza for the site of the capitol building. Construction of the large three-story stone building was started in 1870; the legislators the next year met in the unfinished building which was completed in early 1872. It is open to the public during daytime hours except on Sundays and holidays.

Carson City has other buildings of historic interest. The original federal Carson City Mint, which stamped silver and gold coins for most of the years between 1870 and 1893, is now the Nevada State Museum. It is open during daytime hours except for Sundays and holidays. The many displays are of local lore; mammals and birds in natural desert settings, mineral specimens, baskets and artifacts of local Indian tribes, and other mementoes of early Nevada. One outstanding exhibit is a replica of an underground mine with more than 300 feet of tunnel. Along it are several animated models and exhibits showing mining equipment of Nevada's silver eras. In the south side of the building is a coin press of the original mint. No one can miss the steam locomotive outside of the museum.

On East Stewart Street is the large, block-long building which once had the machine shops of the Virginia & Truckee Railroad. It is presently not open for public inspection. The V. & T., as it was called, last ran in 1950 after serving the Carson City area for more than eighty years.

The Warren Engine Company museum, which stands at Curry and Musser Streets, has historic fire fighting equipment. Carson City still maintains what is the West's oldest continually operating volunteer fire department. The Warren museum is free but open in the afternoons only.

Old mansions abound and are more numerous on streets immediately west of Carson Street and north of King Street. The Rinckel Mansion, the Bliss Mansion, and the Governor's Mansion will interest lovers of late 19th century and early 20th century architecture.

On the opposite page a Virginia & Truckee train is crossing Carson Street, Carson City's main thoroughfare, at a point just north of the present Nevada State Museum, shown at left when it was an assay office. Carson City has many old fine mansions; the above photo identifies some of the pretty girls who lived in the town in 1896.

The three-story brown sandstone state capitol building (below) with its silver cupola is shown only a few years after its completion in 1871. Much of the rock was quarried from the Nevada State Prison, three miles east. In later years, around World War I, wings were built on both the north and south ends of the building.

Nevada's first permanent white settlement centered at this 20 x 40 double logged structure in the early 1850's. It burned in 1911, but a reconstruction built before 1950 is one of Nevada's more popular museums. The huge shoulder of Genoa Peak, mantled with snow and dotted with pine trees, dominates the background. The skeletal limbs of Lombardy poplar trees rise behind the old trading post. Genoa's main street (below) early in this century shows from the left a Masonic hall, a store, and (just to the right of the flag pole) a two-story brick courthouse which is now a museum.

Genoa

Nevada's oldest community is Genoa, 3 miles west of US 395 at a point 12-½ miles south of Carson City. This tiny and silent town of about eighty persons is so close to the foot of the towering Sierra that it is in shadow early in the afternoon. In 1850 some Mormons founded a trading station one mile north of present Genoa. In the next few years several others took up small farms and ranches in the surrounding valley. The young settlement called Mormon Station prospered because of the heavy emigrant travel to California. By 1854 the territorial government of Utah created Carson County to embrace the settlement (Utah maintained jurisdiction until 1861).

In 1856 the townsite of Genoa was surveyed. But after 1857 Genoa became a non-Mormon town when Brigham Young's faithful sold their property and returned to Utah. With fine agricultural and grazing advantages, Genoa by the decade's end had 200 citizens who supported a weekly newspaper, stores, hotels, and a telegraph office. Sawmills and flour mills operated nearby. A Pony Express station was maintained during 1860-1861. Schools, churches, a town hall, and a courthouse for Nevada's Douglas County were built in the 1860's.

Since then the town has prospered by remaining staid and conservative. A few businesses, including a bar (alleged to be Nevada's oldest) are operating. A replica of the original Mormon stockade is a fine museum; it is open daily during the daytime hours. Also situated amid modern buildings are an old courthouse and an early day graveyard. There is the rest place of "Snowshoe" Thompson, who carried the mail over the Sierra to Placerville before the completion of a telegraph line.

For more information on Genoa and old pictures of this and other nearby ghost towns, see the author's *Nevada Ghost Towns & Mining Camps*, available at many stores in western Nevada.

East of Carson City

South of US 50 at a point 3-1/4 miles east of Carson City is a delightful graded loop road. It leads to the Carson River, follows it for about 4-1/2 miles and rejoins US 50 at a point 8 miles east of Carson City. For most of the way, the traveler is on the old grade of the Virginia & Truckee Railroad. Along the Carson River canyon are the foundations of large silver mills that operated especially during the 1860's and 1870's. Though the canyon is quiet today, its steep sides and colorful barren cliffs a hundred years ago echoed the thundering noise of the mills, whose tall chimneys belched smoke high into the air and machinery hissed steam almost 24 hours a day.

Twelve miles east of Carson City is Dayton, a charming historic town which now has only a few hundred people. It was here in 1851 at the mouth of Gold Canyon that California-bound emigrants discovered the first gold in modern Nevada. During the next nine years an army of placer miners from California washed the surface gravel in the streams and creeks of Gold Canyon for free gold. By the time the Civil War started, Dayton had been founded near the mining activity. The town grew fast, and by 1865 its population of 2500 worked in farming, freighting, and milling ore brought down from Virginia City. Even today, there is still much evidence of the mining and milling. Also remaining from the boom era are a school which dates back to 1864, a sagging wooden church, and many brick and wooden commercial and residential buildings.

A mile north of US 50 at a point three miles northeast of Dayton is the ghost town of Sutro. A century ago it had a weekly newspaper, a school, and a variety of small businesses serving several hundred inhabitants. A platted townsite had two parks (dead trees and stumps now mark the locations).

This spot has figured in several history books because Sutro was at the mouth of the famous Sutro Tunnel. It was an enormous project which was designed to drain water from the mines at Virginia City, five miles away and 1800 feet higher, and to ventilate them at a depth of 1200 feet below the surface of the earth. Mr. Sutro envisioned the beginning of a second "bonanza" after the tunnel was completed in 1879. But by then the mines had begun to decline in mineral output. Today the town of Sutro can be visualized through the wooden buildings that remain near the entrance to the unprofitable tunnel.

Located at the mouth of historic Gold Canyon, Dayton ranks closely behind Genoa as the state's oldest settlement. During the days of the Comstock boom, 1860-1878, this town served as a busy transshipping point for Virginia City. This Union Hotel, busy for decades after its opening in the business section of Dayton early in the 1870's, is now a residence. The hearse and the hack are from Virginia City.

In the late 1860's, when the danger of fire and excessive heat and hot water became apparent in the deep ore bodies of the Comstock Lode, California emigrant Adolph Sutro began constructing a five mile tunnel to intersect the mines at about the 1200 foot level. The entrance, shown on the opposite page, is now barred. The people are part of an excursion party.

Dominating the town of Sutro is the founder's Victorian mansion, at right. Note the tree-lined main street. The tunnel entrance is in the lower right, out of the view of the camera.

After 1881, narrow-gauge trains of the Carson & Colorado Railroad passed through Dayton on their way to and from the mining camps of southwestern Nevada. The depot (below) is now a residence. During most of its history, Dayton has had a large foreign born population which included Irish, Italian and Oriental.

1885.

SUTRO TUNNEL
Commenced Oct. 19' 1869.

Tahoe—"Lake of the Sky"

One of the world's most celebrated lakes is 35 miles southwest of Reno via US 395 and State Route 27. It is 16 miles from Carson City using US 50. Glassy blue Tahoe is 6200 feet above sea level in the heart of the majestic Sierra. The surrounding heavily wooded mountains that enclose the lake (it is 21-½ miles long and generally 12 miles wide) reach altitudes of more than 11,200 feet.

The lake's history dates from 1844, when explorer John C. Fremont first saw its waters when on his second expeditionary trip through the West. To Fremont it was Mountain Lake, but it acquired the cumbersome names of Lake Bonpland and Bigler before assuming its present name in 1863. Authorities are not agreed as to what "tahoe" means.

For the last half of the 19th century, Lake Tahoe bustled with industrial activity. Along its shoreline were logging camps where sawmills prepared lumber to meet the insatiable timber needs of the mines at Virginia City. Logging trains and flumes east of Lake Tahoe carried the timber to Carson City, where waiting cars of the Virginia & Truckee Railroad completed the delivery to Virginia City. In conjunction with this activity, barges and steamboats operated on the lake.

Tahoe's industrial days ended about 1897 and the lake became a lightly used summer resort area. Until about 1940 only a few villages knew the beautiful shoreline. A boom started at the end of World War II, when the lake was simultaneously discovered by real estate men, promoters and gambling casino owners. In the next 25 years they filled Tahoe basin with a composite of skiing runs, motels, shopping centers and resorts. Several campgrounds, picnic areas and trails are provided for the lover of the outdoors. Important points on the Nevada side are:

Incline Village. This is a former lumber town, at the north end of the lake, which got its name from a 4000 foot inclined hydraulic tramway a half mile to the east. Ruins of it still remain. Incline Village is now the legendary home of television's "Bonanza." A frontier town with a museum, the Cartwright's ranch house, a trading post, riding stables and other amusements are here. A nearby 18-hole golf course is a picturesque attraction. During the winter Incline Village has excellent skiing facilities. The few casinos here offer entertainment, though larger clubs and motels are at Crystal Bay, three miles west.

Lake Tahoe Nevada State Park. Four miles south of Incline Village and seven miles north of Spooner Summit (on US 50) is Sand Harbor Beach, where swimming and picnic areas are open during the spring and summer. Boating is not permitted here. At Nevada Beach, a little more than a mile south of Sand Harbor, are campsites and facilities for outdoorsmen that are open from late spring until the end of summer.

Glenbrook. This modern village 15 miles west of Carson City on US 50 has a 9-hole golf course, motels and stores. In the 1870's this town of 400 had two first-class hotels and four sawmills. They

fed cut lumber to a logging railroad which ran eastward and up to Spooner Summit on modern US 50. When the last of the sawmills shut down just before 1900, the railroad was dismantled, and the rails were used in the building of another logging railroad on the other side of the lake. Nearby is Shakespeare Rock, a bold cliff with ridges, fissures and color patches which at a distance combine to form a profile of the immortal poet's face.

Cave Rock. Modern US 50 passes through this rock at a point 4 miles south of Glenbrook. This cave, eighty feet deep, is the mythical home of the blue bearded giant of the Sierra.

Zephyr Cove. A mile beyond Cave Rock is this resort area with a large campground. At the office of the Tahoe-Douglas Chamber of Commerce (Box 401, Zephyr Cove, Nevada 89448), you can get detailed information about Lake Tahoe's many resorts and recreational areas.

Nevada State Beach. This pine-shaded recreational area is between Zephyr Cove and Stateline. Here is a campground and a picnic area with an excellent beach.

Stateline. Here 11 miles south of Glenbrook are full resort facilities, including ski slopes, gambling casinos, and hotels with theatre-restaurants. Showtimes are at 1 p.m. for dinner and at midnight for the late show (reservations are required). Immediately beyond the state line in California is the city of South Lake Tahoe. Complete shopping centers, motels, beaches, campsites and the 18-hole Edgewood-Tahoe golf course are found there.

When steamers were operating on Lake Tahoe during the decade around 1900, they stood idle for more than half of each year. In the spring and summer months, the Tahoe regularly left Glenbrook on the east side of the lake, traveled south past Cave Rock, Zephyr Cove, Emerald Bay and Rubicon Point before steaming into Tahoe City, on the California side of the lake. Mail was brought from there to Glenbrook. Lumbering was another Lake Tahoe industry. Ox teams (top, opposite page) moved the logs from the forests on the Sierra Nevada. The first sawmill was built at Glenbrook in 1861. By 1875 the sawmill shown here and nearby mills had an annual capacity of about 25 million feet of sawed lumber. The building with the cupola is the Lakeshore House which is now part of the modern Glenbrook Inn. On the left edge of the picture is the engine house of a nine mile narrow-gauge logging railroad which carried lumber to Spooner Summit (on modern U. S. 50). From there, flumes and the Virginia & Truckee Railroad completed the delivery to the Comstock.

HAULING LOGS — 1876 — LAKE TAHOE

Virginia City—"Queen of the Comstock"

To reach this internationally known mining town from Reno, drive 9-½ miles south on US 395 and then 13-½ miles east on State Route 17. As you ascend into the mountains on route 17, also known as the new Geiger Grade, segments of the old Geiger toll road originally built in 1860 are still to be seen. On that historic road was a never ending series of events: races involving stagecoaches and mounted mail express riders, numerous robberies, and accidents when coaches and wagons and coaches tumbled down the steep canyonsides.

From Geiger Lookout at a point 5 miles along route 17, the Sierra Nevada, Mount Rose, valleys to the south, and the city of Reno all combine for a spectacular view. Geiger Summit is reached on the 9th mile from US 395; east of there is the site of the famous Lousetown Race Track, a Virginia City sportsmen's hangout and now a ghost town. After another 4 ½ miles, Virginia City suddenly appears on the steep eastern slope of Mount Davidson.

Virginia City was the West's largest old-time mining metropolis. Popular writers have told and retold stories of Virginia City early gunfighting and mine speculation years, but the post-Civil War contribution by the Comstock as an industrial center and influence on the national economy generally has been neglected.

Miners washing gravel for gold in nearby streams made initial discoveries in June 1859. Considerable prospecting, promotion and mill building followed during the next five years, and Virginia City's first boom peaked in 1864. Mineral production thereafter fell until the discovery and development of the deep-lying silver ore body, the "Big Bonanza," early in the 1870's. During the next several years the Consolidated Virginia mine produced more than $105 million.

In 1875 Virginia City had more than 110 saloons, four banks, twenty laundries, six churches, more than fifty stores of general merchandise, and both public and private schools. The Daily *Territorial Enterprise*, Nevada's first and most influential newspaper, had nation-wide circulation. But in 1878 a decline set in after the exhaustion of high-grade ore bodies on the Comstock Lode. Though the glory days were over, various small

A photographer captured Virginia City from the water flume high above town in about 1879. Mills and shaft houses of Comstock mines are at the right.

companies sytematically worked lower-grade veins for the next six decades.

Many buildings of historic interest still stand. The Fourth Ward School, Odd Fellow's Hall, and several 19th century commercial brick buildings (including one used by the *Territorial Enterprise*), remain on C Street. Above it are old residences, the famous Piper's Opera House, and the Storey County Courthouse. In the lower end of town below C Street is St. Mary's of the Mountains Catholic Church, an Episcopal Church, office of the Savage mine, residence of John Mackay (one of four Comstock Bonanza Kings), cemeteries with numerous interesting gravestones, and large glory holes created during later mining. Numerous souvenir shops and old-time saloons line the main street. Museums charge only small fees to enter. In the winter a majority of the attractions are closed.

From Virginia City, several short side roads extend in every direction. High-centered cars may return to Reno by way of the Ophir grade, a semi-improved road which leads west from Virginia City to Washoe Valley. That road in the early 1860's was filled with long-line teams and wagons hauling supplies and lumber to the Comstock and carrying ore to mills in Washoe Valley. At a point two miles west on the road, the ruins of an abandoned water flume appear just below the road. Further down in the flat are concrete ruins of an ill-fated milling adventure of the 1920's. Thereafter the road begins a breathtaking descent, especially when driven late in the afternoon when long shadows extend upon the terrain.

Two paved roads lead south from Virginia City. A mile south on State Route 80 is the rival town of Gold Hill which prospered at the lower end of the Comstock Lode during the boom of 1859-1878. When only two years old, Gold Hill already contained many large fire proof buildings. A visitor described the town as an "active, lively place being constantly thronged with heavy wagons hauling in lumber, fuel, goods, machinery, etc., or carrying away quartz to the mills. The roar of the numerous steam mills never ceases, or are operations suspended for a moment, except on the Sabbath." Population peaked in the mid-1870's at about 8000, but after 1878 the town's fortunes were like those of a sinking ship—it was only a matter of time when all would go under. In recent years new residences have been built amid older buildings and extensive mine dumps.

Two miles south of Gold Hill on State Route 80 is the Devil's Gate. Near those rocky crags a century ago was a toll station. Immediately beyond is Silver City, another 19th century Comstock mining and milling town. It was the scene of early gold mining before the Comstock silver discovery of 1859. Silver City always was a low-grade camp.

From the north end of Virginia City, a graded road leads east down Six Mile Canyon, a historic area which once contained silver mills, mines and many residences. Along this charming byway are many places to stop and hike. At the canyon's mouth, watch for a road leading west to the old town of Sutro (see page 11 for description and history).

Some of the miners on the Comstock Lode worked more than 3000 feet below ground level.

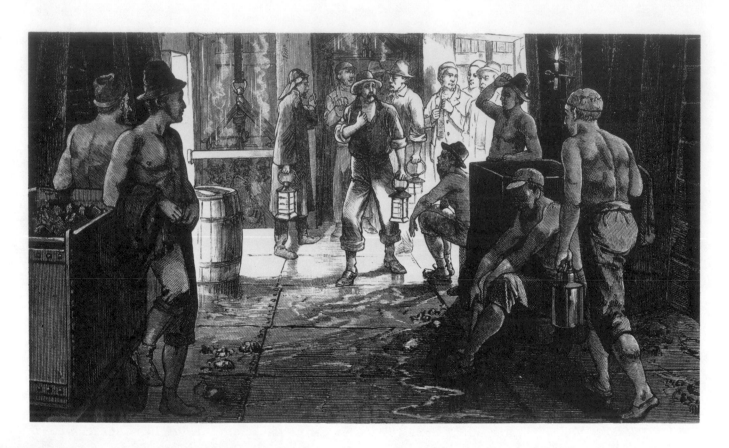

Silver! The romance of the Comstock Lode lured New York newspaper editor Frank Leslie in 1877. Above is the landing in a shaft 1,500 feet below Virginia City. The miner at left is "picking" silver. Other miners (below) prepare to be hoisted to the surface or are about to move ore cars. The men worked in shifts of eight to ten hours, seldom enjoying a day off. Wages averaged four dollars a day.

Early in 1873 the Consolidated Virginia Silver Mine was the scene of the discovery of the deep-lying Big Bonanza, ultimately a producer of about $105 million in ore. It was owned by the Comstock's "Big Four"—John W. Mackay, James C. Flood, James G. Fair, and William S. O'Brien. The mine already was internationally famous when Leslie visited it in 1877 while touring the West. He saw ore being washed in one of the mills at Virginia City (above left). The workers in the above view are manipulating the silver amalgam and distilling the quicksilver in the retort house. In the assay office (below) bullion is being melted and molded. All of these wood engravings of Comstock mining and milling (except the bottom view on the opposite page) were reproduced in Leslie's Illustrated Newspaper.

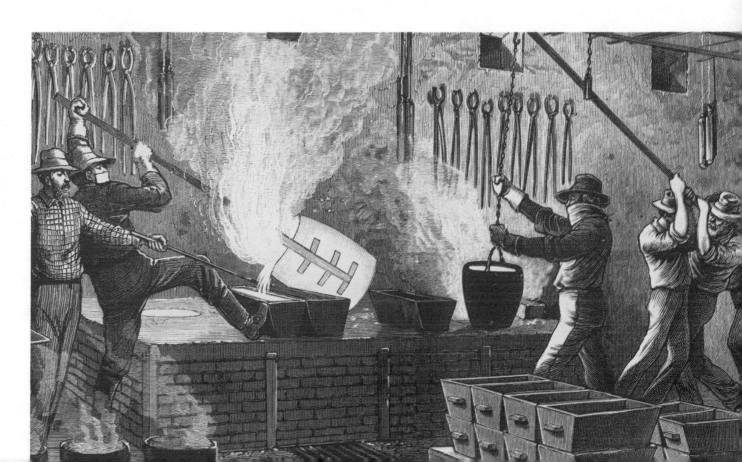

Desert Tour: East of Reno

Wadsworth, 30 miles east of Reno and just off Interstate 80, is a former railroad division point which is now reduced to a village of many ramshackle houses and abandoned buildings. Many occupied residences, a store, a post office and antique shops remain open. Wadsworth will satisfy as an example of rural Nevada, complete with a swinging bridge across the Truckee River.

A nearby ghost town is Olinghouse, 5-½ miles west of State Route 34 at a point 2 miles north of Wadsworth. Gold was rediscovered in Olinghouse Canyon in 1897, and during peak boom periods in the next few years hundreds of people came and went. In 1907 the district had a six-mile long narrow gauge railroad which ran from the mines at Olinghouse to a big fifty-stamp mill one mile west of Wadsworth. Its foundation is still evident, as is the old railroad grade.

Three miles east of Wadsworth on US 95-A is Fernley, a small town with some tourist facilities. Thirteen miles south of Fernley on US 95-A is Silver Springs, the gateway to Lake Lahontan State Park. Silver Springs has only modest accommodations for the tourist.

Formed in the early 1900's when the Lahontan Dam began to impound the waters of the Carson River for irrigation purposes under the Truckee-Carson Irrigation Project, Lake Lahontan now also provides an excellent cottonwood-shaded locale for camping, fishing, picnicking, and boating. To reach Silver Springs Beach, travel three miles south of Silver Springs on US 95-A and then two miles east on a county road. A small fee is charged for use of boating facilities there.

On the south side of US 50 at a point seven miles east of Silver Springs is another boating area. Three miles further (or 10 miles east of Silver Springs) is still another campground, situated just below Lahontan Dam itself.

For Churchill State Park, a half-mile west of US 95-A at a point eight miles south of Silver Springs, was Nevada's largest and most important cavalry post. Indian raids on emigrant trains, interruption of mail riders, and destruction of small settlements led to the establishment of Fort Churchill in 1860. Nevada's first post lasted only ten years, when the army abandoned it. Besides being a state park, Fort Churchill is also a national historic landmark. In addition to an excellent visitor's center, crumbling adobe walls of fort buildings await the traveler. Delightful campsites are maintained alongside the nearby Carson River.

Wadsworth, a busy 19th century railroad and freighting community, is quiet today. The Truckee River flows peacefully through the east end of town, and the Columbus Hotel (above) long has stopped providing a room for the night for stage passengers headed for central Nevada and its mines. With adobe buildings built on stone foundations, Fort Churchill (opposite page) was intended to be a permanent post. All structures were erected on a square facing a central parade ground. These and other brown adobe walls that rise above the sagebrush landscape still mark the arrangement of the old fort.

Wilderness Tour: North of Reno

In a setting of rough precipitous mountains, Pyramid Lake, 32 miles northeast of Reno on State Route 33, has held a certain fascination for visitors since its discovery in January 1844 by John C. Fremont on his second expedition. While Kit Carson and Fremont were reconnoitering in the area, they came upon a sheet of green water about twenty miles long. Fremont wrote that it broke upon their eyes like the ocean. Ascending a nearby peak, Fremont's party sat for a long while enjoying the view, for by then everyone "had become fatigued with mountains, and the free expanse of moving waves was very grateful."

The men noted a very remarkable rock formation in the lake's center. "It rose . . . 600 feet above the water and, from the point we viewed it, presented a pretty exact outline of the great pyramid of Cheops. This striking feature suggested a name for the lake, and I called it Pyramid Lake."

A Paiute Indian Reservation bearing the same name now embraces the entire lake. It is noted for excellent cut-throat trout fishing and boating. The "pinnacles," a series of unusual tufa formations at the lake's north end, and the Indian Sphinx rock formation are other points of interest.

The town of Gerlach, 105 miles north of Reno, is the base for desert travelers in search of remote areas to explore. For the following places, inquire at Gerlach about latest road conditions.

Hardin City, a ghost town 45 miles north-north-east of Gerlach via desert roads, dates from the 1860's when a mining rush took place to the Black Rock Desert. The nearby hills were blanketed with claims and three silver mills were erected on the basis of false assays. The town lasted but three years. As a reminder of that fiasco are the stone walls of the mills.

The Fly Ranch Geyser is a half mile east of Sate Route 34 at a point 24 miles north of Gerlach. This is a fountain of recent origin. When a local rancher drilled a well in 1919, he inadvertently struck a body of highly mineralized water. Over the years the minerals have built up a fountain more than twenty feet high. At intervals of about a minute, water surges from the top of the cone and cascades over the sides, constantly renewing its bright orange-lime colors. An endless supply of mineralized water assures the future growth of this unique fountain.

About 10 miles further north, or a mile west of State Route 34 at a point 37 miles north of Gerlach, is the ghost mining camp of Leadville. All that remains of this 20th century development are a few wooden buildings. The view from the Leadville mine high above the valley is breathtaking. Even further north, rugged places such as Little High Rock Canyon and Summit Lake await the experienced desert traveler.

Unusual rock formations (above) abound at various places on the shore-line of Nevada's largest lake. During each summer thousands of Pelicans inhabit Anahoe Island, a national wildlife refuge in Pyramid Lake. Paiute Indians (opposite page) are herding cattle with 63 different brands.

In January 1844 John C. Fremont's expedition arrived at Pyramid Lake and camped opposite "a very remarkable rock" which rose more than 600 feet above the water. The pyramid had attracted their attention for many miles. In the foreground left is Fremont's party, a few of their horses and mules, and the expedition's twelve-pound howitzer mounted on a carriage.

PYRAMID LAKE

Sierra Tour: West of Reno

Verdi, just north of Interstate 80 at a point 11 miles west of Reno, was a prosperous sawmill town and minor resort area late in the last century and early in this century. Motels, restaurants and stores are still open. From here several delightful back roads lead past modern residences and wilderness areas.

Near Verdi in November 1870 occurred the West's first transcontinental train holdup. Seven robbers boarded the east-bound train, cut off the engine, mail and express cars from the rest of the train, and made the engineer run the train to a nearby culvert where the rest of the gang was waiting with tools. Treasure boxes were opened and about $41,600 stolen. Though the gang successfully split up after hastily dividing the money, the law soon found the trail. All were caught in a few days. Two men turned state's evidence and most of the money was recovered. All others in the gang served long prison sentences.

West of Reno 33 miles on Interstate 80 is Donner lake, located near a camping area of the ill-fated Donner party which perished in sudden early snows while attempting to cross the Sierra in 1846. Fishing, boating, and sightseeing long have been popular in this resort area.

Shown here is the upper end of Donner Lake, 3½ miles by one mile, the "Gem of the Sierra", according to an early Pacific Coast tourist guide. Clearly visible are snow sheds on the wooded mountains. "Were it not for the occasional rattling of cars on the mountainside," an early observer noted, "one would fancy that he was in one of nature's secret retreats, where man had not ventured before."

When the Central Pacific Railroad was being built across eastern California and northern Nevada in 1867-69, Verdi came into being as a lumber town which supplied ties to the railroad. Shown above is an early 20th century sawmill. The little Shay on standard-gauge rails is dumping freshly cut timber into the pond, from which a conveyor belt feeds the logs directly into the mill, as the closeup view shows.

The box factory was built in late 1902 and employed about four dozen men. It is hard to believe that Verdi once had such diversified industries.

Points of Interest in Reno

University of Nevada: Built on rolling hills at the north edge of the city is the Reno campus of the University of Nevada. It is so typical of small universities that motion picture producers have used the 193-acre, tree-studded campus as a setting for full-length movies about college life. Old buildings blend with modernistic new ones, and peaceful Manzanita Lake and the landscaped grounds are good subjects for pictures.

The Mackay School of Mines Museum: In the center of the campus is the fine museum which contains many exhibits of Nevada's mining history. Mineral specimens of the state are shown with explanatory notes. Large panoramic views of Nevada boom towns show early architecture, mines, mills and smelters of the bygone era. The museum is open during the daytime, Monday through Friday.

Nevada State Historical Society: This state operated museum-library is located at the north edge of the University of Nevada at 1650 North Virginia Street. Old maps, books, boomtown newspapers and other reference materials that trace Nevada's history are available for public use. There are exhibits showing interior home furnishings, mannequins clothed in early fashions, Indian baskets and artifacts, mineral specimens and other mementos of Nevada's past. A courteous and knowledgable staff will answer your questions about old Nevada. There is no admission charge. It is open during daylight hours except Sunday and holidays.

Fleischmann Atmospherium-Planetarium: Directly across from the Nevada Historical Society is this facility which is used to study atmospheric phenomena. In summertime 45-minute programs are offered daily in the afternoon and early evening; in winter the schedule is more limited. A science exhibition hall and a ten-inch reflecting telescope also are under the big saddle-shaped structure. Call the University of Nevada for program times and further information. There is a small admission charge to the show.

Washoe County Library: Located on 301 South Center Street in downtown Reno, this award-winning library is nationally renowned for its modern interior architecture. Integrated among the lounge areas and periodical and newspaper shelves are many large shrubs and trees. The library is open throughout the day and evening, Monday through Friday. It is on a more limited schedule on Saturday and Sunday and is closed on holidays.

Pioneer Theatre Auditorium: Opened in 1967 on the site of the old state building and park, this sunken modernistic structure on South Virginia between Mill and State streets, is a convention favorite.

Centennial Coliseum: This facility at South Virginia Street and Kietzke Lane opened in 1964, when Nevada celebrated its 100th year as a state. It is larger than the Pioneer Auditorium and can handle trade shows, circuses, rodeos, ice shows and other sporting events.

North Virginia Street Gambling District: In the very heart of the city, on and adjacent to Virginia Street, in Reno's glittering casino district. At the north end is the famous arch with its slogan, "Biggest Little City in the World". Action goes on 24 hours a day, seven days a week; top entertainers perform in the theatre-restaurants at the 8 p.m. dinner shows and again at midnight. Reservations are required. Less elaborate lounge shows play from early evening into the small hours of the morning.

Harold's Club Antique Gun Display: On the casino's second floor is a collection of some 2000 weapons. These include dueling pistols, custom and hand-made, famous Deringers, Winchesters and Colts, as well as a smaller collection of spears and shields. The display is open at all times, though children are permitted only in morning hours until lunch time. No admission is charged and special guided tours can be arranged.

Harrah's Automobile Collection: Located in suburban Sparks is the world's largest and finest collection of antique, vintage and classic automobiles. More than a thousand gleaming cars are on display. The collection also has other types of transportation, cycles, boats, a few airplanes and an antique steam locomotive. Visitors see the shop areas where skilled craftsmen rebuild automobiles to original factory specifications. It is open during daylight hours. Call or visit Harrah's Reno casino for tickets and for times of free transportation from downtown Reno.

Parks

Wingfield Park: In the heart of downtown Reno, adjacent to Arlington Avenue and on the south side of the Truckee River, is the park which is named for a prominent Nevada businessman. Children's playgrounds, tennis courts and fountains have been built into handsome landscaping.

Whitaker Park: Bounded by Ralston, Washington, University and Seventh Streets, this park is named for the founder of a school that operated on the site in the 19th century. The attractive playgrounds are shaded by many trees.

Idlewild Park: This 48-acre park is Reno's largest; it is about a mile west of the center of the city and adjacent to Reno High School. Baseball diamonds, a children's playground, a swimming pool, two lakes, a fish hatchery, and a small zoo, are in a tree-shaded setting on the south bank of the Truckee River.

Paradise Park: Located on Oddie Boulevard, just east of Silverada Boulevard, this park has picnic grounds and a large lake offering fishing and sail boating.

Virginia Lake: Along Lakeside Drive at a point one half mile south of Plumb Lane is the park that centers on a lake. It has become the home of hundreds of wild ducks and geese. It offers fishing as well as picnic areas and a children's playground.

Reno Scenic Drive: Reno's outstanding points of interest are located on a specially designated route which leads past the University of Nevada, through fine residential areas, through the downtown gaming area and borders agricultural districts, local schools and parks. The drive takes about 2½ hours, and signs are posted along the route.

TRUCKEE RIVER RENO NEV.

A Pictorial History of Reno

Reno was founded on a warm sunny spring day, May 9, 1868, when the Central Pacific (now the Southern Pacific) Railroad, auctioned off 400 lots in a neatly marked townsite on the north side of the Truckee River in what is now downtown Reno. At that time the surrounding Truckee Meadows contained only a few small farms. Myron Lake had built a toll bridge over the river and a small wayside inn next to it (on the present site of the Riverside Hotel–. Through most of the 1860's the settlement was known quite properly as Lake's Crossing.

The illustration above shows Lake's inn and bridge in 1862, six years before the founding. Lake maintained both to serve an increasing number of Californians headed for the rich Comstock Lode at Virginia City (behind the Virginia Range in the background left). During the 1860's the crossing was the funnel for pack trains, for animal-drawn freighters, footpackers and horsemen, all in a rush to get to the great silver land at Virginia City.

Lake's well known roadhouse had a bar in front and dining room and sleeping rooms in back. A complete meal cost fifty cents. Through the mid-1860's Lake grew rich in the dull business of supplying food and rooms to passers-by in search of silver. Every time someone crossed his wooden bridge he collected a toll—fifty cents from every horseman, a dollar for each carriage, a dollar and quarter for a large wagon. He also acquired considerable adjoining acreage in the lush Truckee Meadows.

No city could be more one man's idea. Early in 1868, Lake realized that soon his land would be on the nation's first transcontinental line. Moving eastward from California, an army of 4000 Chinese, with surveyors, engineers, and railroad personnel, would end their construction of the Central Pacific at Promontory, Utah, in May 1869. Seeing opportunity, Lake approached Charles Crocker of the Central Pacific in March 1968 with an offer. He would give the railroad eighty acres of his sage-covered meadows if the railroad would lay out a townsite, build its main western Nevada depot in the middle of the town, and deed back to Lake alternate lots.

Crocker agreed and in April 1868 the town was platted on the north side of the Truckee River. On May 4, the

Central Pacific tracks reached the site of the future town, next to Lake's inn. Five days later the townsite, located in the ranching area in the right background beyond the famous bridge, was auctioned before a crowd of more than a thousand. Bidders came from northern California and Western Nevada and, particularly the Comstock.

Crocker had named the town "Reno" but his reasons have produced argument. Some say that "Reno" was a name drawn by lot from a box in which railroad officials had contributed suggestions. One newspaper reported, deadpan, that the word was easy to write. It is known that the city was named for a Virginia Civil War loyalist, Jesse Lee Reno (not to be confused with Major Marcus Albert Reno of the Custer disaster), who rose to Major General on the Union side before he fell in battle in 1862.

The fate of Lake's original inn, and of the wooden bridge, is shown in the photo at right, taken about 1879. Reno had become the county seat and its taxpayers had built a fine, two-story court house. Lake's original inn (shown above) burned in 1869 but he rebuilt and, on New Year's Day, 1870, he opened the commodious hotel known as the Lake House. It was renamed the Riverside fifteen years later, and it continued as a landmark until 1906, when again it was entirely rebuilt.

The bridge had a different fate. Lake continued to collect tolls until his bridge franchise expired in 1871. The county then made it a free bridge despite Lake's strenuous objections and an unsuccessful appeal to the State Supreme Court to maintain possession. After 1877, the Truckee River was spanned by the iron bridge shown below. In 1905 it was replaced by the concrete bridge of today.

The story of a hotel and a bridge.

. . . and in ninety years.

During the 1870's Reno grew fast as the supply and distribution depot for western Nevada and eastern California, especially Virginia City. At the same time it suffered the usual boomtown scourges of fire and crime. The 1880 census showed that Reno was still a stepchild of Virginia City and its suburb, Gold Hill. It had less than an eighth of the combined population of the bonanza towns.

By 1882-83, when the panorama (left above) was taken, Reno had a commercial district with varied businesses for a town of about 1400 people. Its main thoroughfare, Virginia Street, ran southward from the railroad tracks. Barnett's store, at right, at the corner of Commercial Row, claimed to have the state's largest, cheapest and best stock of boots, shoes and men's hats. Silhouetted at the end of the street is the Lake House, and behind it, with its tall cupola, is the courthouse.

An identical modern view shows the famous Reno arch in the immediate foreground.

The description of Reno reproduced below is taken from a transcontinental railroad tourist guide published in 1880.

Reno—is 7.64 miles from Vista; is the county seat of Washo county, and contains a population of about 1,500. It was named in honor of General Reno, who was killed at the battle of South Mountain. This city has rapidly improved within the last six years, and now contains five church edifices, two banks, a fine court-house, a number of good business blocks, a steam fire department, several small factories, two daily newspapers, the *Journal* and the *Gazette*, and is the distributing point for an enormous freighting business to the north, as well as the south. Some good agricultural land surrounds the town, as well as many herds of cattle and sheep. The State Agricultural grounds are located here, in which is a very fine race track. The Lake House is the principal hotel.

The greatest mining region in the world is reached via Reno. Virginia City, located over the mountain to the southeast, from this station is *only* 21 miles distant, by the old wagon road, but by rail it is 52 miles. Before the completion of this road, Virginia City was reached by stage, over a fearfully steep zig-zag mountain road, but the difference between the "old and the new" is more than made up in the comfort of the passage if not in time.

At the time when these stages were running to convey passengers, a fast "Pony Express" was run for the purpose of carrying Wells, Fargo & Co.'s letter bags. This pony express was once a great institution. When it left Reno, the traveler could have observed that the mail express bags were thrown from the cars before the train had ceased its motion. By watching the proceedings still further he would see that they are transferred to the backs of stout horses, already bestrode by light, wiry riders. In a moment all is ready, and away they dash under whip and spur to the next station, when, changing horses, they are off again. Three relays of horses were used, and some "good time" was often made by these riders.

By the late 1880's, Reno looked like a charming little country town, as seen from what is now Whitaker Park. The town also was a shipping point to California for Nevada beef and agricultural products.

With its conspicuous tower, the famous Navada Bank (below) dominates Reno's business district around 1890. Other fire-proof buildings contained attractive retail stores and shops, commodious hotels and saloons. In that day, tree-lined North Virginia Street (shown in the background) had many fine residences. Note the hitching posts. The wooden sidewalks had doors that opened outward to allow supplies to be lowered into the basements of stores.

Late in the last century, T. K. Hymers operated a livery stable (above) near the corner of Second and Virginia Streets.

The office of the Nevada State Journal, a Reno daily published since November 1870, was housed with two other businesses.

The Lake Mansion at South Virginia and California streets is surrounded by extensive gardens. The walkway from the left leads to granite steps behind the bicycle and a six-foot porch that had hand-carved ornamental piers and balusters. The basic material is California redwood. Evidence of a New England influence is shown in the quoined house corners that have alternating lengths of uneven blocks and the ten foot square "widow's walk" on top of the hip roof. (In New England folklore the seagoer's wife could watch for the returning ship and start the meal when it was sighted). This building was once in downtown Reno but in 1972 it was moved next to the Centennial Colesium on South Virginia Street.

After the turn of the century, Reno came out of its dullness which had existed since the decline of the Comstock Lode, about 1880. The development of new mines, especially at Tonopah, Goldfield and other central Nevada mining camps after 1903, meant growth for Reno. Its population soon doubled, and before 1910 Reno had 10,000 people. A Virginia & Truckee train is in the station of the Southern Pacific depot (above). Note the black engine and shiny brass and canary yellow freight cars. In the right foreground is a shuttle bus which met the trains and took visitors to the hotels. The driver sat with the baggage in front. The horse-drawn dray at left carried freight and express.

An important suburb of Reno is Sparks which emerged in 1904 as a division point for the Southern Pacific Railroad. Shown here is the roundhouse then under construction. Its shops could handle locomotive service and repair of any size.

Below is the Virginia & Truckee bridge which crossed the river to the east of downtown Reno.

Jeffries
vs
Johnson

Reno's big excitement early in this century was the Jim Jeffries-Jack Johnson world's heavyweight championship fight on June 4, 1910. It was dubbed "the battle of the century." Railroad side tracks were jammed with Pullman sleepers to accommodate the overflow straw-hatted crowd. All hotels had been booked for weeks, and most had to provide sleeping cots in the hallways. A hastily erected hexagonal arena with a capacity of about 15,000 was erected on East Fourth Street, midway between Reno and Sparks. The Boilermaker Jeffries (left), the 10-6 favorite and the former heavyweight champion, looks for an opening. Some sport fans called him "the Great White Hope." But the black Johnson became the new champion by outfighting and outgaming his older opponent, wearing him down and finally knocking him out in the fifteenth round. Promoter "Tex" Rickard made big money on this fight in Reno, yet the future held for him million dollar gates in the East.

At Center and Commercial Row (above) autos and horse-drawn vehicles mingle with the immense throng of fight fans. A transition in transportation is evident. All numbered seats as advertised (below) were sold. At ringside (top, opposite page) the fighters are sparring for an opening. In the clench scene (lower left), Jeffries is hanging on. In between rounds and at his corner, Jeffries welcomes a rest for his wobbly legs.

No.63. The Crowd at the Ringside. Reno, July 4.

No.65. Jeffries-Johnson

The Reno Stock Brokerage Company had its office in the Golden Hotel Block on Center Street. A Thomas Flyer is shown in this view of about 1909.

The Riverside Hotel (below) had a lanai where society ladies played cards. Street cars ran south on Virginia and Plumas Streets to Moana Park until Service was discontinued in 1927.

On the east side of Virginia Street in the early 1900's, on the present site of Harold's Club, is the Frank Brother's Liquor Store. The proprietors look ready for action. In the bottom view, the driver has just backed his wagon toward the store entrance to discharge his load of wine barrels from California.

N. VIRGINIA ST. RENO. NEV.

A WINTER NIGHT

"UNIVERSITY OF NEVADA" - RENO

In the 1920's Reno bustled as a great trading and banking center for most of Nevada north of Goldfield, as well as for California towns east of the Sierra. The automobile made it possible for thousands to motor into Reno to vary their social life and shop for seasonal goods. Virginia Street was a thoroughfare of well-apportioned stores offering goods for distinction and quality. Far down the street is the original Reno arch, built in 1927 for the Transcontinental Highway Exposition. Two years later, the advertisement of the exposition was removed and in its place the city's famous slogan was installed.

From an opposite view (below), on a wintery night, the arch bears the famous slogan which was chosen in the summer of 1929 after a $100 contest. No other city in the nation has exploited a slogan to such good advantage.

The University of Nevada, an entity provided for in the original 1864 state constitution, initially was established a decade later in Elko. By 1885 it was moved to Reno. Beginning with Morrill Hall, buildings were gradually added, including Lincoln Hall, the men's dormitory in the center of the picture. Manzanita Lake is in the foreground.

In the 1920's Blanche Field (below) was located in southwest Reno, at the present site of the Washoe County golf course. In front of the hanger is a U. S. mail plane.

Popular in the mining camps, faro was still an attraction at Reno clubs in the 1930's, although it is seldom played today. Players sat stoically around the tables and watched the turn of the cards for hours.

Gambling was first legalized in Nevada in 1879. Thirty years later, in 1909, a vote was taken to decide whether gambling should be abolished. The reformers won, and in 1910 gambling was outlawed. In the next decades changes in the law made gambling intermittently legal or illegal. Generally the gambling business also benefited as changes in the divorce law shortened the residence requirement. Since 1931, gambling has been fully legalized and through the 1930's the gambling, plus the liberal divorce law, gave Reno a heavy divorce business. The population of Reno's divorce colony in the 1930's varied in proportion to the national prosperity. Many of the restless visitors putting in their residence time took to the diversions of the roulette wheel, the tumble of dice, and the flip-flap of cards at the faro and poker tables.

46

Converted from an old farm house west of Reno, the Willows was a fashionable night club of the 1920's and 1930's. Reno's socialites mingled with wealthy visitors from other states. Shown above is roulette. Higher stakes were allowed in private clubrooms at the rear (not shown). In downtown Reno, the Bank Club (below) featured chuck-a-luck, a game that has lost popularity since the 1930's. Reno Mayor E. E. Roberts stands behind the cage.

Although Reno had been caught up in boom of the roaring 20's, the bank failures of 1929 dampened the spirit of the town. But when gambling was legalized two years later Reno took advantage of the new liberal law and continued a steady growth until 1940. The census that year showed 21,317 inhabitants. Nearby Stead Air Force Base contributed greatly to the town's economy during World WarII and to a lesser degree in the two decades that followed. Great casinos were built and the area's natural resources were exploited for recreational purposes. Skiing and boating especially became popular. Since mid-century energetic Reno continued with a rapidly developing economy. It is more diversified than its better known sister to the south, Las Vegas. Reno has known more than a century of growth since the auction on that spring day in May 1868.